The Ten-Digit Poet

Robert E. Blackwell

PublishAmerica
Baltimore

© 2004 by Robert E. Blackwell.
All rights reserved. No part of this book may be reproduced, stored in a retrieval system, or transmitted in any form or by any means without the prior written permission of the publishers, except by a reviewer who may quote brief passages in a review to be printed in a newspaper, magazine, or journal.

First printing

ISBN: 1-4137-3753-6
PUBLISHED BY PUBLISHAMERICA, LLLP
www.publishamerica.com
Baltimore

Printed in the United States of America

Dedication

To God, from whom all inspirations flow,
My mother, without whom I couldn't grow,
My teachers from school, who planted the seed,
My family, whose love is all I need,
Our dog, whose woofs and licks are a treasure,
My friends, for whom writing is a pleasure,
And the world, whose wonders of work and play
Give me new things to write about each day.

The Ten-Digit Poet

I have a most peculiar obsession
That plays out when I set forth words in rhyme;
Each and every topic and impression
Conforms to ten syllables every time.

I've tried to write other forms of fashion,
But somehow, it just never seems to fit;
It seems I can only keep my passion
When I count off ten syllables, then quit.

Have mercy on the Ten-Digit Poet…
Addicted to decasyllabic rhyme,
So one-dimensional…yes, I know it…
But don't rescue me, 'cause it feels sublime.

Imagine my maddening circumstance…
If you can while keeping your sanity;
Try to fit all music with the same dance,
Or whatever else suits your vanity.

If I'd budget wealth like I do each line,
I'd have a bank account fit for a king;
Yet, my verse is all that is truly mine
To laugh, cry, dance, or make music to sing.

Thus, the tale of the Ten-Digit Poet
Is done, and I've kept my obsession true:
This gift I share, as only I know it…
One finger times eight plus one thumb times two.

Faith and Service

A Poet's Prayer

Lord, before you tuck me in for the night,
Grant my fingers another verse to write;
While I sleep, pour wisdom into my mind,
And let my waking words heal humankind.

Gift me once again to see through your eyes…
To drink deeply the beauty of your skies,
To follow the rainbow's eternal beams,
And paint words from the canvas of my dreams.

When conflict strikes the world, I'll bear the strife
With thoughts that calm the chaos of this life;
When sorrow fills my loved ones, I will cry
With words as tears like raindrops from the sky.

Give me the sweet laughter of silly rhymes
To give every soul some light-hearted times;
Give me also the soft pillow of prose
To lull the world into Sleepyland's throes.

Lord, before you grant me eternal rest,
Let me bless the world as I have been blessed:
With the words to express the peace and love
That comes from you, in Heaven high above.

Does God See Color?

Does God see color? Some say He doesn't,
And therefore, we should all be color-blind;
Yet, His creation has a vast rainbow
Of people of color of every kind.

Was it always this way? Back in the day,
The world was one race that spoke the same words,
But by divine design, we grew apart,
And throughout the world, we scattered like birds.

Through the years, the world's people multiplied,
And our once-common language disappeared;
Isolated in our clans and cultures,
We learned that differences should be feared.

Our differences have many aspects,
Such as gender, creed or religious sect;
In this day and age, the hue of one's skin
Is the difference that we least respect.

It is the most visible difference;
This makes it the easiest to assume
Whatever stereotypes we adopt
When someone "different" enters the room.

It colors our very first impressions
And governs the tone of our reactions,
Giving each person more of a reason
To distrust all future interactions.

Does God see color? I say that He does,
But He does not judge by it like we do;
Instead, it is through the heart and the mind
That He knows the truth about me and you.

We would benefit from this example:
Instead of looking for "color-blindness,"
Try learning from all our differences
And bridging them with mutual kindness.

Good Morning, My Friend

Good morning, my Friend; I know you are near,
Although I can't see you, touch you, or hear,
I feel in my heart (as always the case)
That your Presence is near in every case.

You've blessed me again with another day,
So I may go forth as you show the way
To contentment, peace, and ongoing love,
Showered upon me from your home above.

I've no idea why you love me so well,
Being one born of dust shaped in this mortal shell;
I've no idea why you adopted me,
Or moved me from bondage to liberty.

All that I know, and all I can say,
Is: I love you so much, in every way;
For all that I have, for all I can be;
I owe everything to your love for me.

Guide me onward as I travel the path
Through Life, with its pitfalls and worldly wrath;
Within your love, I will surely abide
From now 'til the day we'll walk side by side.

Heaven's Gate

INTRODUCTION

The morning sky is hidden by gray clouds
That hide the sun and makes the breezes cold;
The barren land shivers, and I with it,
Feeling the sting more now that I've grown old.

There must have been a time when I knew warmth;
Sometime in my youth, I knew how to fly,
But my wings have been clipped and now I walk,
Not knowing if the sun's still in the sky.

When I'm not walking, I sit by the road
And ponder the eternal question "Why?"
I used to watch the birds, but now I don't
Because seeing them always makes me cry.

Throughout the day I walk, and sit and think,
That question like still waters running deep;
The nights bring memories relayed in dreams
That drive the question home during my sleep.

Yet I sleep in an effort to forget
The day I flew away from Heaven's Gate;
I wish for dawn, to awaken and walk,
And ponder not the question of my fate.

PART ONE – DEPARTURE

I hadn't walked these streets in quite awhile
(It has been a time, times, and half a time);
Not that I could ever become concerned,
Or worry when I hear the hour chime.

When I left here, it never crossed my mind
That I would ever decide to come back...
There was no reason I wanted to stay,
And where I went, no comforts did I lack.

But looking from a cloud beyond the skies,
I saw it looked so beautiful and green;
I began to covet its loveliness,
And my longing for its treasures was keen.

My brothers saw the gleaming in my eyes
And begged me with tears not to go away;
Despite their pleadings I did not listen,
But said my goodbyes, for I would not stay.

Away I flew through many golden streets
Until at last I passed through Heaven's Gate;
I found the object of my many dreams,
And sought the fantasies I wished to sate.

PART TWO – PINNACLE

I stopped flying so I could walk with men,
Believing I would always have my wings;
I learned to use the "wisdom of the wise,"
And sing the songs a child of the earth sings.

I wrestled for the comforts that I sought,
And justified myself that it was right;
I wore a blindfold and saw illusions
By which I told others they had no sight.

I polished my halo with earthly wax
So they'd marvel at how brightly it gleamed;
In my quests I became very "rich"
With earthly wealth far beyond what I'd dreamed.

What a life! I ignored all the storm clouds,
And pretended the sun was always out;
Even the rain didn't bother me much,
Nor did thunder and lightning produce doubt.

I did not bother to open my eyes
And see the mourning inside Heaven's Gate,
Or I'd have known that the rain was angels' tears,
The thunder proclaiming my now-lost state.

INTERLUDE

Once in awhile, the sun shines through the clouds,
And I dare to find hope in golden rays;
Just as quickly it fades, and I recall
The rest of my story of darkened days.

PART THREE – OPPOSITION

I discovered (as I did once before)
That the earth's treasures are fleeting at best;
In my own hands, I had none for support
But myself when I needed to find rest.

Soon my days of favor with men had ceased…
Others came, claiming heavenly power;
Suddenly, I became one in a pack
Of men chasing the wind every hour.

Everything became nothing so quickly,
And I was stripped, my shame exposed to all;
I was beaten for what little I had
And discarded in some forsaken hall.

Angry and wounded, I made up my mind
To fly straight away, back through Heaven's Gate,
But my new antagonists clipped my wings
And left me lying in my sorry state.

PART FOUR – FUTILITY

With human effort, I picked myself up
Amid the laughter of cruel voices;
Mouths without faces mocked and demeaned me…
Me! I once was the people's first choice!

Now, they drove me away through city streets…
To the despondent outskirts they took me,
Daring me to try again to reclaim
The fame and glory that belonged to me.

They left me, laughing, to make my own way
On a planet turned hostile with Man's hate;
I suddenly felt the chill of the winds
And the rains that fell at a steady rate.

I beheld broken wings once great and proud
And believed I would heal and fly away;
The seasons have come, gone, and come again,
And I've been grounded to this very day.

I then realized how far removed I was
From the home I had inside Heaven's Gate…
From the fellowship of the Family,
And the freedom from oppression and hate.

PART FIVE – OSTRACISM

Since that time, I have walked through desolate towns
And endless stretches of lonely highways;
I keep searching for friends to walk with me,
But they're not to be found on the by-ways.

Even the villages shutter their doors
Against me (can't they see I mean no harm?);
Those in the streets hide their faces from me,
But their eyes fill with horror and alarm.

I try to share with them my odyssey
As a warning to leave this world behind;
They mock me and retort: "What would you know?
You demented man…you're out of your mind!

"You're unclothed and unwashed, blind in both eyes,
Yet dare to instruct us and swear it's true!
How can you lead us to something better?
We declare our filth less despised than you!

"If it's so much better, why did you leave
That so-called paradise past Heaven's Gate?
You vagrant; go spin your tale somewhere else;
We have no concern for your sorry fate!"

They send me away without the least stitch
Or morsel, or droplet to ease my throat;
My feet and legs ache from walking the miles,
And my body shivers without a coat.

PART SIX – DESPAIR

What men do by day, my dreams do at night:
Torment me (though asleep, I cry with grief)
With memories of all of my transgressions
Together, without a hope of relief.

Some nights I decide not to sleep at all,
And I walk through the hills in search of peace;
Even then, my comfort's not guaranteed
In a world in which nightmares never cease.

At times I wish that my Father would come
And look for me on this lifeless ball;
I question whether He knows I am here,
Or if He even cares for me at all.

I look upward, but no longer see
The land of contentment past Heaven's Gate;
I stray between hope that they'll take me back,
And despair that my longing comes too late.

PART SEVEN – REFLECTIONS

Still, I live, and the world is still standing
(Such as it is…I feel I don't belong);
They can't hurt me further; I hurt myself
In my appetites for everything wrong.

It is still the Father's world, after all,
And it was not made without its treasures…
Indeed, they're both majestic and simple;
They were created for proper pleasures.

There are some in which I can find a smile:
Sunrises announcing another day;
Clouds that make images filling the skies;
Rainbows whose colors are cheerful and gay.

I find enjoyment in counting the stars,
Or watching leaves in a breeze as they spin;
When the earth sleeps underneath its white quilt,
I try matching a snowflake with its twin.

But these are a poor substitute at best
For the loveliness inside Heaven's Gate;
I try to remember what it looked like,
But the distance of time and space is great.

PART EIGHT – OBSERVATIONS

I watch as the earth's beauties are ravaged
By people whose thirst cannot be sated;
For them only power is absolute
And all truths are meant to be debated.

Their god is Power, and they are faithful
To its worship (they practice what they preach);
They are men who define their own wisdom,
And raise children gifted in what they teach.

One robs his brother to pay off his friend;
Another spits in his mother's eye;
Parents claim devils made them kill their sons,
And angels made them watch their daughters die.

They all claim one space and live in conflict
Disputing…contending what they believe;
I hang my head shamefully in pity
And question the spirits that they received.

If only I could have my wings restored,
I could show them the way to Heaven's Gate.
But, could I save them? Can I save myself
From suffering as we await our fate?

PART NINE – LESSONS

I will fail if I depend on myself
(I know, because I have tried it before);
I was guided by my wants and "wisdom"
And I thought I could attain so much more.

I have chased the most meaningless of winds
And now I am mortal, destined to die;
So long have I grieved over my mistakes
I have run out of tears with which to cry.

But, I must believe that Somewhere beyond,
Is the home where exists nary a care;
And I must believe that Someone above
Is waiting to find me and take me there.

PART TEN – REPENTANCE

I tried to return the same way I left:
In arrogant self-righteousness and pride,
But now I will do whatever it takes
To find Home – where Truth and Peace abide.

If I cannot fly, I'll gladly walk
And I won't stop 'til I reach Heaven's Gate;
I'll bring whoever wants to come with me…
Any who wants to escape this world's fate.

Life in the World

During a winter evening's indulgence,
I am playing a game found in a book,
Where I must find the best path through the rooms;
The task isn't as easy as it looks.

While I'm exploring this puzzle, I find
That it's not wise to trust all of the clues,
And after awhile, I put it aside;
The frustration is giving me the blues!

I discovered an interesting parallel
Between the puzzle and this present life:
Each of us must discover the best path,
And most of the "clues" bring nothing but strife.

Life in the world is a challenging maze,
And it's so easy to steer yourself wrong;
Each twist and turn causes more of a daze
As the puzzle of Life goes on and on.

There's an additional riddle to solve
Once you've managed to emerge from the haze;
Both riddle and answer are found through clues
That you find while you're exploring the maze.

Clever, Life! Discontent with one puzzle;
Always willing to throw us still more curves
Without thought or care for those in your web
Or regret for the siege upon one's nerves!

Through the mirages, the ruses and traps,
A solution exists…yes, it is true!
It cannot be found in Life's conundrums…
Those crafty dilemmas disguised as clues.

The solution is a wonderful Friend,
Who straightens out the most twisted pathway;
He answers every riddle with the Word,
And dispels shadows with the Light of day.

Yes, Life in the world is a tangled maze,
But, take heart…now, you can find the way out:
Seek Life with the Friend…escape the riddles,
And escape the life of darkness and doubt.

Mother Of Exiles

A lady stands in solitary place
Upon an island, looking toward the coast;
Serenity adorns her lovely face
As she stands vigil at her lonely post.

She holds a torch lit brightly in her hand,
To shine a light upon the peaceful shore;
Her crown a symbol of each far-off land
To whom she opens wide the golden door.

"Mother of Exiles, in silence you speak
To every soul in every tongue on Earth;
A message heard from every mountain peak
That reaffirms humanity's great worth."

Her love is an open invitation
To those of every culture, every race,
No matter one's wealth or social station;
She offers every soul an equal place.

She speaks all languages from silent lips,
Her goal to bring the masses to her side;
There's no brighter beacon to weary ships
Than the lady standing amidst the tide.

"Mother of Exiles, may God keep you near,
And let your light shine over every shore;
May your love fill our children's hearts with cheer,
And our own hearts with love forevermore."

One In The Spirit

It all began with a fateful tower
That the masses felt compelled to create;
To the heavens was its destination,
And for themselves, there was a name to make.

But the Lord, in his infinite wisdom,
Chose to thwart this selfish, capricious plan;
He confused their tongues and divided them,
And sent diverse people across the land.

Millennia hence, in a "modern" world,
Crowded society clamors for space;
We've avoided togetherness for so long
That now, it's a concept that's out of place.

"Number One" must be extremely happy
Because we all look out for him so well,
And thus the world is now a place too cold…
Too cruel in which the meek and mild can dwell.

BUT…just as the Tower of Babel fell,
So must society's walls be torn down
By giving love freely to every soul,
And spreading the sweet truth of Peace around.

Consider that the greatest sacrifice
Was a gift of unconditional love…
A sweet covenant of a second chance,
Giv'n all by the Almighty above.

SO…let us all be one in the Spirit…
Let us all join our souls, and minds, and heart;
Let us bring together new harmony
Instead of living as people apart.

Let us love others as we love ourselves…
There can't possibly be a better way;
We can then rejoin what was separate
And together await the coming day.

Song #7

Amidst the ebb and flow of life I stand,
Breathing in the springtime that has spread over the land;
No matter if I've seen it all before,
The sights and sounds delight me and my spirit soars.

The Artist is at work: He paints a scene
Of April rain and blossoms that splash upon the green;
With rainbows in the puddles of the street
To add contrast to the grayness where earth and sky meet.

I'm walking by myself, but not alone,
For I hear voices from within that are not my own;
And as I walk past fields of grass and grain,
I listen to the chatter of voices in the rain:

"Behold the sun, doing what it does best:
Bathing the earth in golden light, moving east to west;
Its heat is tempered by the breeze's kiss
That blows and swirls around; it flies from that point to this.

"Behold the flowers dancing with the trees:
All of them provided for, they live a life of ease;
They're watered by the rivers of the plain
That run to seas (that never fill) and return again.

"All of these things happen year after year,
And every turn of the world brings a laugh and a tear;
So, what else is new? What else can be done
To make living less boring under light of the sun?"

As I walk onward, the clouds fill the sky,
Growing darker with the doubts of my wondering why;
I battle my thoughts; what strength can I muster?
I can feel that the Earth has lost some of its luster.

In prayer, I ask God to ease my mind,
To take away the depression of my thoughts unkind;
Then the turmoil of my mind fades away,
And the voices speak again; there is a lot to say:

"The sun arises and life begins anew…
All of God's creatures thrive beneath a sky of blue;
The eagles fly, the robins sing aloud,
And lions roam their vast domains, standing firm and proud.

"The lilies earn no wage, nor spin a wheel…
And yet, are they left naked, without hope or appeal?
The rains fall; with love, the earth is trimmed clean,
With rainbows left as ribbons to decorate the scene.

"Even if what has been will be again,
The wonder of life goes on, never dull or inane;
Seedtime and harvest on earth will endure,
And the miracles of Life will remain fresh and pure."

While resting in the branches of a tree,
It is with love I marvel at the beauty I see:
The splendor of the mountains far away…
The peaceful valleys giving love and comfort each day.

The shadows of afternoon grow and spread…
The sun mellows in the sky from gold to ruby red;
The early bird seeks refuge in its nest,
And all creation settles down for the evening's rest.

I turn back to the friendly shores of home,
Content that Heaven's beauty will shine where'er I roam;
Those voices are now silent, but in thought,
Waiting for a new day to see what it has brought.

The Spinning Wheel

I saw a wheel in the corner, spinning
Threads in a rainbow of diverse sizes;
I'm told it was there from the beginning,
And the wheel can be full of surprises.

I wonder, what makes it go? I don't know,
Or if there's an answer, it's escaped me;
Must be the Spinner above, I suppose…
Making the world what He wants it to be.

I walked to the wheel and picked up a thread
From the collection piled up on the floor;
It could have come from a quilt on a bed…
There were patterns of colors, and much more!

Another I picked up wasn't as long
As the first, and no two threads were the same;
What was the purpose? All seemed to belong,
And I saw that each was given a name.

Who named them, or cut their lengths? I don't know,
Or if there's an answer, it's escaped me;
Must be the Spinner above, I suppose…
Making the world what He wants it to be.

Now some of the threads are pink at the head,
While blue decorates all of the others;
The colors tell a story for each thread,
Telling apart sisters from their brothers.

As each one spins longer, the colors change
Like the trees at the passing of seasons;
Only the Spinner determines each change,
Unfettered by Man's search for the reasons.

When each thread reaches its determined length,
It is cut from the wheel by hands unseen,
A gentle touch by hands of an awesome strength;
The thread is complete…a miracle scene.

I looked at the thread I hold in my hand,
And noticed a silver tip at the end;
I knew that this thread had a life long and grand,
For each one had its share of blessings sent.

Most wonder how it's done, and most don't know,
But an answer is there for all to see:
The Spinner above is making it go…
Making the world what He wants it to be.

What's Left

Take away the joy of thoughts free and pure…
What's left is an empty, imprisoned mind.
Stripped of confidence, it wanders, unsure;
Deprived of incentive, it becomes blind.

Take away the beauty of love expressed…
What's left is a broken, imprisoned heart.
Like a winter tree, it stands undressed;
Its life, like the leaves scattered far apart.

Take away the hope of eternal life…
What's left is a barren, imprisoned soul.
Deprived of God, given over to strife;
It is swallowed up in Hell's darkest hole.

You Can See It in Their Eyes

I watch politicians proselytize
The people they're trying to hypnotize;
Yet, they sought out the devil's compromise,
Trading their honor for Ambition's prize.

Is it obvious, they're telling us lies?
Indeed so…you can see it in their eyes.

I listen to radio jocks chastise
All dissenting thinkers under the guise
Of loving America, freedom fries,
And let's not forget those sweet apple pies.

Did they forget why the brave soldier dies?
Indeed so…you can see it in their eyes.

Nocturnal seductresses tantalize
The men who desire to say their "goodbyes"
To loneliness, seeking the best surprise
That a working man's shrinking dollar buys.

Does the heart feel the pain the mind denies?
Indeed so…you can see it in their eyes.

Only the love of a just God supplies
The means to soothe the pain and calm the cries
Of whosoever will look to the skies
And seek wisdom beyond the "earthly wise."

Do the angels smile when a saved soul dies?
Indeed so…you can see it in their eyes.

Reflections

A Scribe's Wisdom

Do not condemn, but lift no helping hand.
Do not destroy and leave a barren land.
Do not scorn lost skill, but refuse to teach.
Do not set goals beyond a person's reach.

Do not inflict wounds you refuse to heal.
Do not punish when anger's what you feel.
Do not curse darkness, but light no candle.
Load no burdens you refuse to handle.

At another's expense, one cannot thrive;
Life needs us all to be friends to survive.

A Tear

A tear of sorrow for the loss of life,
Another of anger at endless strife;
One more for our children's innocence lost…
Who can place a value on such a cost?

Yet, a tear of hope this darkness will cease,
And of thankfulness for freedom and peace;
And lastly, a tear for justice and love
For the nation and world 'neath God above.

Angry Voices

I hear the voices while trying to sleep…
At first quiet, then rising as they fail
To hide the anger that's bubbling from deep
Within the shattered hopes of their hearts' veil.

Why do they fight at the end of the day?
Most likely finances that have gone sour;
Maybe it's cooking, or chores – who's to say?
All I know is, it gets worse by the hour.

He blames her for having no cash to spend…
She blames him for drinking 'til he can't see;
I love them both, and on them I depend…
Have they no clue what their fights do to me?

What if it's me that they're fighting about?
Were they this unhappy before my life?
If I go away, it might cleanse all doubt
If I were the cause of all of their strife.

But, where would I go, and how would I live?
I don't think I'll get too far on my own;
I'll just have to hope someday they'll forgive
What I've done, and they'll keep me 'til I'm grown.

Those angry voices are quiet for now,
But sleep for me is a long time away;
I sure hope that God above will allow
That tomorrow will be a better day.

Cocoon

Being a butterfly's overrated…
Nothing to show for my evolution
But the brittle remains of my singed wings,
The result of Nature's cruel collusion.

I no longer have it in me to dream
Of reaching for an unreachable moon;
I'll retreat to my abandoned refuge:
The long-broken fibers of my cocoon.

What is left of my wings will compensate
For the breach I made during my escape;
Closing my eyes, I'll trade maturity
For the innocence I had taking shape.

Being a butterfly's overrated…
I shouldn't have sought to grow up so soon;
I'll now drink from the cup of delusion
While hiding inside my broken cocoon.

Footprints Unseen

The morning snow blanketed the dark streets
And every step that I took was muffled;
The flakes descended from the sky in sheets,
Denying my stride…and thus, I shuffled.

I reached a shopping center parking lot,
Where my stride was safe, though I couldn't sprint;
I startled myself with a sudden thought:
Despite the snow, I left not one footprint.

And yet, while invisible to my eyes,
I believe that my steps were surely felt,
If only by the lot 'neath snowy skies…
That empty…lifeless…silent…asphalt belt.

The heart also feels a friend's unseen path,
Rejoicing for the bond with kindred soul;
Yet, when broken, there is sadness…and wrath…
For the wound that leaves an eternal hole.

Thus, for every hole left by a lost friend,
Footprints lead to and from that wounded place;
Time may soothe the bond that came to an end,
And fate may find a soul to fill the space.

The footprints of friends who have come and gone
Will be felt and matched by the heart's soft beat;
Whether dusk, twilight, or a new day's dawn,
One will always feel the patter of feet.

Lessons Learned
(after September 11, 2001)

I will never forget the destruction;
In my mind's eye, I'll always see the storm
While a country pursues reconstruction
And a nation must redefine the norm.

I re-learn the lesson taught oft-before
Of life, and death, and also of re-birth:
To love, laugh, and thrive, in peace and in war,
And in each soul to find something of worth.

I've learned to wave: both a flag in the sky,
And a hand to a friend I've yet to make;
To find heroes in those who march and fly,
And in those who give time for others' sake.

I've learned that dying for hate is a shame,
But living for love is a better life;
I've learned there is heartache in seeking fame,
But slaves to peace are yet masters of strife.

So many lessons a spirit must learn;
So fleeting is the time to learn them all.
As I grow older, I will always yearn
For new wisdom each day…both great and small.

Song #14

It's safe to say we all love sunny days,
And we turn up our noses at the rain;
When it falls, we wish it to go away,
As though raining is society's bane.

We handle relationships the same way:
Blue skies and sunshine are what we love best;
Conflict is something to be avoided
Because it puts our friendship to the test.

A land that receives only the sun's rays
Will soon suffer the ravages of drought;
It needs rain for cleansing and nourishment,
Which causes the seedlings within to sprout.

Conflicts with loved ones are storms of the soul:
We thunder in anger, and rain in tears;
Thus cleansed and nourished, renewed love blossoms,
And such growth draws us nearer through the years.

Therefore, delight in the storms of Nature,
And even more in the storms of the soul;
The former replenishes all the earth,
And the latter makes every spirit whole.

Paper Plane

While sitting at the canvas of this page,
I waited for my muse to speak to me
According to such whims she might fancy,
In any shape or fashion they might be.

The sheet of paper lay upon my desk...
A virgin, never touched by pen and ink;
Yet eager to receive such caresses
Of whatever thoughts my brain chose to think.

My fingers, too impatient for my muse,
Took up the blank page in a playful hold;
Then they brought the edges close together
And creased down the middle into a fold.

One fold led to many, then many more,
Until the page that awaited my words
Became transformed into a paper plane
That flew out the window to join the birds.

The plane flew high
Into the sky,
Floating with ease
On morning breeze,
Having no care

Gliding through air,
Looping, swirling,
Sailing, twirling,
Sublime its flight,
Dreamy the sight,
Feeling the wind
Making it spin,
Finally night,
Ending its flight,
Coming to land
Into my hand....

I contemplated my well-traveled plane,
And noticed a difference in the page;
Unfolding the sheet, I saw evidence
Of quite an evolutionary stage.

Lines of phrases in neatly wrapped verses
Became a present that tickled me pink;
My muse, amused, wrote a poem with my plane
And sent it to me with a smile and wink.

In retrospect, all of my random thoughts
Are paper planes flying within my brain;
Their landings transform into the wisdom
That God and my muse wish for me to gain.

What, you may ask, did I do with this page?
I have passed it along to share with you;
Let your muse soar high in a paper plane,
And believe in the gift it brings to you.

The Chase

I was running, but had no direction…
Just the need to reach the safety of home;
My pursuers, dark shadows of the night,
Followed me as I desperately roam.

I ran though my legs lost their energy,
Otherwise stopping would have meant my doom;
Their purpose of pursuit a mystery
Which added much to my own sense of gloom.

Each time I glanced back, the shadows were there,
Never closing in or fading away;
The night bore silent witness to this scene
Of them, the pursuers, and me, the prey.

The streets were familiar scenes of my past,
Of neighborhoods of my most tender youth;
The houses were moments of my lifetime,
Of learning of life's mysteries and truth.

My eyes remained sharp from desperation
To find a safe haven where I would rest;
My strength declined, and my courage was low…
I feared I would fail this ultimate test.

I reached a deserted intersection
And had no choice but to stop for a break;
My body was spent, and my mind gone mad,
For this chase became more than I could take.

My shadows, my tormentors, approached me,
Their blank faces betraying no feeling;
They knew all along that they would find me,
No matter the paths of my mind's reeling.

They did not apprehend me, as I feared,
But stood at a distance within arm's reach;
I could no longer run, and could not hide,
So I reached out with my hand to beseech.

The shadows which pursued all this time,
Shrank away from the peace I tried to seek;
I was confused, then angry, then forceful
And all at once, I didn't feel as weak.

I stepped once again toward those shadows,
And once again, they retreated from me;
I faced them with new determination
And demanded they give their names to me.

"I am Phobia," said one. "I nurture
Your bad experiences into fears."
"I am Regret," said the other, "I've grown
From all of your failures over the years."

"As long as you've lived, you've tried to avoid
Living up to the weak points of your life;

You've run, but we've followed you everywhere,
Filling your mind and heart with pain and strife."

My anger gave way to introspection…
In choosing to run from my darker days,
All I did was prolong my agonies,
And prevent the sun of Forgiveness' rays

I stepped toward my shadows…one step, then two,
And watched them retreat into the twilight;
I faced them again, and watched them dissolve
Into the glow of the dawn's early light.

Facing one's shadows, while a daunting task,
Can bring a brighter day within one's reach.

Uncharted Streams

Along uncharted streams lies the future,
And we can but imagine what we'll find:
Each mind's eye sees a unique horizon
As a tale with an ending to unwind.

My mind's eye sees multitudes of vistas
To be captured with strokes of ink and pen:
Vistas of perspective…of fantasy…
Of concepts short-lived, and worlds without end.

Blessed are the leaders, who conquered their goals
And attained fulfillment, fortune and fame;
Blessed also are those who conquered the storms
Of their lives…contentment they rightly claim.

Yet, blessed beyond compare are those of us
Who weave quilts of creative thought to share:
The sculptors and singers, actors and scribes
Take the masses away from common cares.

With God's blessings, we create the magic
That reaches the rainbows among the clouds;
Inspired, we open new dimensions
And on strong wings do we soar, free and proud.

We use our gifts to portray the future
According to the visions we've received;
Our children learn lessons about our lives:
What we've learned, and all the things we've believed.

Our uncharted streams will soon become known
To those who take time to follow our course;
In so doing, our hope is to inspire
Others to chart their streams without remorse.

Winter's Dream

Winter's blanket lies heavy upon me,
And I recline on tundra for my bed;
Yet, though covered in ivory splendor,
Do not mistake me for one of the dead.

I sleep…and my dream is a silver mist
That swirls endlessly in each direction;
It fills my eyes with insecurity
And ensures visions escape detection.

I'm blinded by the unknown's white shadows;
My muse roars its silence and deafens me;
The fingers of my heart touch, but can't feel,
And my mind swallows the mist's tasteless sea.

Despite this, I walk in un-straightened paths
To nowhere at all, compelled by the wraith
Of the mist that consumes my sleeping thoughts
And anticipates the death of my faith.

Winter's breath caresses my frozen brow,
Her kiss transforming my heart into ice;
She deepens the barren mist of my dreams
And demands my soul as a ransom price.

I wander onward through my frozen dream,
By will of a faith that's alive, though weak;
I might be blinded, but my faith still sees,
And though deaf, I can still hear its voice speak.

My faith's touch feels those things which I can not,
And finds the taste of visions very sweet;
Thus, I wander through the mists of my dream,
Fearing the unknown fate that I must meet.

After what feels like an eternity,
I feel the cloud in my eyes dissipate;
Before me, distant visions coalesce,
But I know not what to anticipate.

The horizon of my dream takes the form
Of three mountains that stand tall in the sky;
The mist seeks to cover them, but in vain,
And those summits lift my soul very high.

The first mountain is called, "Inspiration,"
And it gives to me the long-lost desire
To plant anew the garden of my mind,
With flowers rekindling forgotten fire.

The second rock is called, "Perseverance,"
And the mountain's surface bears many scars;
Despite them, the mountain stands proud and tall,
Providing a resting place for the stars.

The third mountain does not possess a name,
Its summit is hidden beyond the skies;
I embrace this rock and begin to climb,
To learn which mysteries hide from my eyes.

The mist swirls again, but I disregard
Its appeals to my sensibilities;
Together, my faith and I will explore
My unlimited possibilities.

I climb, and I no longer feel frozen,
As the clouds give way to the morning sun;
The kisses that chilled my soul fade away…
The sleep of my winter will soon be done.

I feel the bed of my sleep softening,
And new tears caress my slumbering being;
Such tears are kisses of newly-bloomed dreams,
Promised with love from the garden of Spring.

Wishes And Dreams

I have a most special, favorite time:
To wish, and dream about thoughts far away;
Life would be sad if I could never wish
Or dream of new worlds…foundations to lay.

For wishes and dreams, like waves on the sea,
Bring much peaceful comfort and joy to me.

I dreamed of a hill…bright, peaceful and green,
With flowers that danced and swayed in the breeze;
I wished to lie there and bask in the sun
Watching the butterflies roam where they please.

My wishes and dreams, like waves on the sea,
Bring much peaceful comfort and joy to me.

I have often dreamed of a flake of snow,
Gliding through the sky upon breaths of air;
I wished to glide with it through tree branches
And over rooftops, away from all cares....

My wishes and dreams, like waves on the sea,
Bring much peaceful comfort and joy to me.

I have dreams each day of an awesome love
Growing stronger with each laugh and each tear;
My wish, in the glow of a dream fulfilled,
Is to keep dreaming this, year after year.

My wishes and dreams, like waves on the sea,
Bring much peaceful comfort and joy to me.

I will cherish my dreams for their treasures,
And keep wishing on stars in skies of blue;
And as long as I live, I will rejoice
For all the times that my wishes came true.

For wishes and dreams, like waves on the sea,
Bring much peaceful comfort and joy to me.

Love and Like

Come What May

Our paths stretch toward unknown horizons,
And is clouded by uncertainty's mists;
Yet, come what may, I'll always walk with you,
No matter how long the unknown persists.

Our days, while oft filled with peaceful sunshine,
Are also fraught with conflict as the norm;
Yet, come what may, I'll fight alongside you
Through all your battles, and all of your storms.

Our lives will be heavy with the burdens
Laid upon us by many so-called "friends;"
Yet, come what may, I'll always help carry
Your burden from dawn until the day ends.

The whims of Fate are often capricious,
Breaking the heart and making the soul groan;
Yet, come what may, my soul will stay with yours,
Thus ensuring you'll never walk alone.

Daddy's Little Buddy

I spy, with a parent's curious eye,
My little buddy playing with his toys…
Building blocks stacked two by two, pretty high;
Such is often the way of little boys.

My oldest son isn't so little now,
But he's my buddy, and always will be;
When I gaze into his eyes, I think "Wow!
Oh, to see life again as he must see."

I remember when I first held him near,
Soft blankets covering his birthday suit;
I recall the first smile and hug so dear
That it rendered all of my burdens moot.

Now, watching him build new worlds in his mind,
I think of all the countless times I've smiled
Because God has chosen to be so kind
As to bless me with the love of a child.

for Christopher

Five Questions For a Lover

When...

...have I last told you how much I love you?
Seems it's been ages since writing my friend;
Eternities since I wrote to my love
To tell her my passions for her will not end....

Where...

...in the heavens did you come to me from?
You must be an angel I've discovered;
With silky hair, and eyes filled with laughter,
It's plain that a treasure I've recovered.

How...

...many times have I dreamed of feeling
The fire of your kisses, your warm embrace?
Together in my dreams...both night and day;
In my heart, you have your own special place.

Why...

...did we meet, and why at this chance moment?
That question's one I have no chance to solve;
I can only enjoy what has blossomed since,
And find joy in watching our love evolve.

What...

...would have happened if we had never met?
Life would be less than it is with you near;
Questions done, I'll reflect on the answers
That equal gratitude for one so dear.

For Ted

Somewhere beyond the silver-azure sky,
I can feel your presence…it's in my heart;
Speaking to me at times, and oft again –
A reminder that we're never apart.

We learned long ago that there's no distance
That can separate the love between us,
And as God willed, our paths intersected
A time or two…I felt that was a plus.

We spent more time apart than together,
But the bond we share is unbreakable.
I said this long ago, and say it today -
My faith in this remains unshakeable.

Somewhere, at different places and times,
I see your face in the dawn's morning sun;
I hear your voice in my own mind's silence,
And feel your touch in the rain when all's done.

Time – that relentlessly flowing river
Moves on, its currents both steady and swift;
I grow older each day, and treasure more
What we've shared…truly, a beautiful gift.

The dusk now gives way to the falling night,
And for now, I'll close my reflections here;
Sleep well, loved one, until the new dawn
Brings the day with its treasures far and near.

*In memory of my brother,
William Theodore Macon
July 18, 1947 – May 27, 1997*

Rescued by a Rainbow

The storms of heartbreak raged in full fury…
Lightning scissors ripped through clouds of lost hope,
Their wounds spilling the rain…a hemorrhage
Testifying to their failure to cope.

This was the weather of my broken soul:
Cold fronts with gale force winds heavy with pain,
Oppressive fog that clouded my vision,
And unceasing torrents of my eyes' rain.

With no shelter for respite from the storms,
The clouds of loneliness fell upon me,
The lightning of unworthy "friends" stung me,
And despair, like the fog, enveloped me.

But you, the rainbow, appeared in my sky…
A promise sent from the angels above,
A pledge of renewal, comfort and peace,
And an omen of blessed, rekindled love.

Your golden beams dispersed Despair's dark fog,
Replacing it with new hope's morning light;
Your blue turned away every cloud of gray,
And filled my sky…it is a precious sight.

Indigo and violet calmed my moods,
And their soothing took away all my tears;
Green beams shone in soft blades of newborn grass,
And their bright optimism chased my fears.

Wrapped in orange trim, you brought me the sun…
Dawn, you called it. I called it a treasure;
Then you painted red streaks throughout my sky,
And Dusk became a most cherished pleasure.

My tears fell again, from all the happiness
At the change in the weather of my soul;
I embraced with eternal tenderness
The rainbow, because you have made me whole.

Song #12

It is pre-dawn, and I walk empty streets;
The pavement witnesses silent foot beats.

I am alone, and yet you are with me.

I carry you with me, to all places,
All hidden corners, and open spaces.

I feel your presence, though none else can see.

The morning sun smiles from the sky above,
As we talk, laugh, and fall deeper in love.

My soul joins with yours, and your heart with mine.

Your love overflows my heart's beating space,
Sending tears of joy down my grateful face.

I'm a dew-kissed flower; you're my sunshine.

Song #13

A word and a quarter-note got married,
And raised children of sentences and tunes;
Music and Poetry became a song,
Whose melody flourished for many moons.

No finer duet can be found on Earth:
Her notes giving voices to each songbird,
And his words of wonderful tales to tell;
It is the most joyful sound to be heard.

Take time to enjoy this wonderful blend
Of art forms joined to form a special bond;
The magic they share is more powerful
Than any sorcerer and magic wand.

A word and a quarter-note got married
And lived on…winter, spring, summer, and fall,
Raising children of tunes and sentences,
And thus singing lullabies to us all.

Song #16

The brisk winter breeze is very chilly,
And it fills all whom it touches with cold;
Yet I'm safe from its bite within the arms
Of the most precious one I have to hold.

Her breath a sweet lullaby in my ear,
Her breasts a soft pillow to rest my head;
Her arms a warm blanket of love and care
That keep me unharmed from all forms of dread.

Her eyes are twin shining, sparkling diamonds
Whose radiance delights all my being;
Her lips are the petals of Spring roses
That convey with each kiss all she's feeling.

Carry me not from my precious love's side…
To no other paradise will I roam;
I'm spending tomorrow and all days hence
Within the sweet arms of my home, sweet home.

The Gotcha Song

My youngest son and I made up a game…
We play it every day and every night;
It may sound somewhat odd, but just the same,
He thinks our game is really quite alright.

The rules are very simple: while I sing
A melody I call the "Gotcha Song,"
I clown around just like a ding-a-ling…
It makes him laugh and want to sing along!

"I gotcha nose," I sing, and gently tweak
My baby's nose, which makes him laugh each time;
He hides his nose, allowing me to sneak
And tug his ear while making up a rhyme.

"I've got an ear…oh, yes; I've got an ear,"
He giggles more, so wound up he can't speak;
I sing again, his laughter ringing near:
"And now, I've got a little rosy cheek!"

We play awhile, until we tire out,
And then it's to settle down for bed;
The laughter in his eyes leaves me no doubt
That we've had fun, when all's been done and said.

With gentle hugs, I wish him a good night,
And tuck him into bed, where he belongs;
I can't wait for the next day's morning light,
When we can sing again our silly songs.

for Timothy

Twin Pathways

Each life travels along a unique path
From one's past towards future tomorrows;
The landmarks are moments within one's life…
Of living and thriving, joy and sorrows.

Life is a map comprised of many paths,
Which travel all possible directions;
Some converge for a time, some intersect,
And some lonely paths have no connections.

There is a blessing that I count daily,
And that is for the path converged with mine;
The soul mate with whom I journey along,
Who turns each day into the sweetest wine.

Together, the path becomes a highway,
And the landmarks we will always cherish;
Every moment of the seasons of Life
Is fresh with love, which will never perish.

The horizon that fills each person's path
Is one filled with great mysteries unknown;
It is the most blessed and happiest soul
Who does not travel that pathway alone.

for Rebecca

Thoughts that Tickle

Fisherman's Lament

Fishing is stupid, and fishing is dumb…
Look at me here: a hook stuck in my thumb,
A nasty ol' burn, because of the sun,
But did I catch fish? Ha! Nary a one!

I drowned all my worms, and then dropped my pole…
I feel myself sinking; the boat has a hole;
The water is leaking in under my butt,
And I sit here stuck in this crazy rut!

When I wake before dawn at four o'clock,
And rush down the road to the nearest dock,
What am I thinking? Where is my brain?
Saturday mornings, I must turn insane!

By noon, my mood has become quite edgy:
You'd be, too, if you had a wet wedgie!
My pole's on the floor of this stupid lake,
And laughing fish is more than I can take!

When I arrive home, I look quite the sight…
My clan knows there'll be no fish fry tonight!
The rest of the weekend is spent in thought
Of how much trouble my hobby has brought.

I know, there's only one thing I can do
To keep future weekends from feeling blue:
To heck with the lake, I'll go to the creek…
I'm sure I will do better there next week!

Interlude

In a room lit only by candlelight,
We share a secret interlude of love,
Our witnesses the shadows of the trees
And soft beams from the twinkling stars above.

Before your eyes, I wave my magic wand,
My eyes locked on yours in adoration;
Your precious bottle dripping from the brim
With trembling, overdue anticipation.

My hand guides my wand inside your bottle,
Plunging gently inside its secret depths;
Then it stirs the liquid your bottle holds
While trying to control my shallow breaths.

Finally, reaching the peak of delight,
I withdraw my wand with little trouble;
Taking a deep breath, I blow at the tip,
Producing a very large…soap bubble.

(Gotcha!)

Looking Glass

I read of Alice and the looking glass…
What a charming tale for Lewis to spin:
A schoolgirl ventures from reality
To fantasy, then reality again.

I have wondered, when viewing a mirror,
About the world on the opposite side;
If Alice explored there by accident,
Then why can't I experience the ride?

The mirror seems simple at the surface,
For the reflection's the only thing there;
But the looking glass could be a doorway
Leading to the world of self…do you dare?

Think of the other side of the mirror:
Speaking with a language that's inside-out;
Pledging allegiance with a hand firmly placed
Where a lung should be breathing in and out.

Imagine taking a drive in your car,
Traveling the other side of the road;
Or think of the sun moving west to east
As the day progresses from new to old.

Ponder the hands of the tock-ticking clock
While it travels from hour to hour;
Going from noon to eleven o'clock
As though enchanted by mystical power.

All of these thoughts brought a smile to my face
As I leisurely straightened up my tie;
With a knowing wink of my left (and right) eye,
I bid my reflection a fond "goodbye."

You'd think I'm crazy to dwell on a world
That I found thriving on my bathroom shelf;
Here's my challenge: gaze at your reflection
And explore the world of the mirrored self.

Random Thoughts

Random Thought #1

"Politics" is an interesting word;
Its lesson in the meaning it teaches:
Poly, from the Latin meaning "many,"
Tics, meaning "thirsty, blood-sucking leeches."

Random Thought #2

Choose carefully whose toes you tread upon;
Otherwise, the deed will bring you sorrow.
The toes you trod today could be attached
To the butt you'll have to kiss tomorrow!

Random Thought #3

The biggest fallacy of human times
Is the well-worn sentence "Those who can't, teach;"
If not for those who educate, who else
Would extend the borders of a child's reach?

Random Thought #4

Despite the rains that fall upon one's life,
I've learned a trick that warms my very soul:
Make some sunshine by smiling through your strife,
And a rainbow appears to make you whole.

Random Thought #5

Reality, when meeting fantasy,
Is often hostile and unforgiving;
Yet, one should embrace one's own world of dreams…
Because one who stops dreaming, stops living.

Random Thought #6 (Free Verse)

It is never the mighty gust of wind
That makes a man remove his coat,
But always the silent warmth of sunshine
That encourages him from his shell.

Random Thought #7

If only Life's road were both straight and flat,
Wouldn't that be more easily traveled?
Wouldn't the horizon's clear view ahead
Make journeys less easily unraveled?

And yet…if it weren't for valleys and peaks,
How fulfilling could such a journey be?
Without curves, detours, and forks in the road,
Would we discover all there is to see?

Random Thought #8

Majorities rule a democracy;
There's no better example, in my hunch,
Than that of four wolves and one single lamb
Casting their votes on what to have for lunch.

Mythical Heroes

The Bard's Tale

Have harp, will travel…but even without,
I'll get by on my wits to cheer the crowd;
Weaving tales or magic, there is no doubt
I can take away every heart's dark cloud.

I have no house, and yet I am home
Wherever I lay my head for the night,
The pursuit of Life compels me to roam…
An apple from which I must take a bite.

While it may seem that I might have no cares,
Take heed…not all of my life is a lark;
I do have the means to protect my shares
From those who believe me an easy mark.

My satin glove conceals a fist of steel
With which to smash an opponent's resolve;
I know some magic…I can either heal,
Or cause an evil one's will to dissolve.

I'd rather trade tales than swings of a blade,
So I keep my skin thick and temper strong;
Whether a capital or forest glade,
You'll find me happily singing a song.

When the show's over, please drop me a coin,
Or bring me a tankard o'er which to nurse;
Perhaps better yet, I'll simply un-join
Some ungrateful curmudgeon from his purse.

As long as there's someone to entertain,
You'll find me with a song or tale to tell
To add to your joy, subtract from your pain,
And lighten your heart so that all is well.

The Druid's Tale

I am the moon, who guards your dreams with care,
And I'm also the sun, who keeps you warm.
When happy, I'm the soft breeze through your hair,
But when angry, beware; I am the storm.

I am Nature; thus, I am everywhere:
The proudest rock of the highest mountain;
The liveliest leaps of the tiny hare;
The coolest splash of a river's fountain.

I am a Mother; the milk of my breast
Is the rain that nurtures the farmer's field;
My quilt is the snow's flakes, tenderly dressed
To cover the fallows and keep them sealed.

I have given birth to each blade of grass,
And guided the paths of each new flower;
I bring sleep to souls when it's time to pass
From Life's minute to Eternity's hour.

This world is my cradle…treat it with care,
And it will sustain you all of your days;
With rain for abundant harvest to share,
A moon's gentle beams and a sun's bright rays.

The Paladin's Tale

The tower bell's echoes rang in the breeze
As I approached the manor on the plain;
I'd heard tales of the baron's life of ease,
And more rumors of his ill-gotten gain.

The drawbridge and the gate were open wide,
Extending to me an invitation;
Yet, intuition struck me once inside,
That my skills would face initiation.

The portcullis met the ground in a rush;
There'd be no turning back…the game's begun!
The voices around me fell to a hush,
And dark clouds surrounded the noonday sun.

In the courtyard, I saw the baron's throne,
And the figure upon it filled with glee;
His guardsmen were animated from bone,
And a young dragon towered over me.

"Welcome to my humble domain, young squire…
We were hoping a new playmate would drop by;
I hope you'll give us the sport we require,
Then for dinner my pet will have squire pie!"

"Well met, foul demon; I know it is you
Who slew the baron and took on his guise;
Thus, I will render to you your due,
And your demons, like you, will feed the flies!"

The skeleton warriors surrounded me,
Their eye sockets scarlet pinpoints of hate;
Beyond their number, I did plainly see
The "baron" anticipating my fate.

I wielded a sword of the Spirit's might,
And a shield of faith in my God's power;
Facing these awful creatures of the night,
My salvation was my helm this dark hour.

The horde charged forward…I met them head on,
Carving Righteousness' path through fleshless bone,
'Til the last of the skeletons was gone,
Sent back to the pits from which they were grown.

The dragon arose and flew toward the sky,
Scorching nearby clouds with its brimstone rain;
In menacing circles did this beast fly,
His countenance meant to cause fatal pain.

With the breastplate of truth about my chest,
The beast's true form I was given to see;
Incensed at my calm in facing this test,
The dragon roared, and flew to devour me.

The roar became shrill, with terrible screams,
Yet I gave no ground to this delusion;
Swinging my sword, I reflected sun beams
That dissipated this foul illusion.

The demon within the baron attacked,
Leaving behind the noble's lifeless shell;
He aimed to harass, annoy and distract,
Overwhelm, destroy, and send me to Hell.

His weapon was the hopeless fate of Man,
Embodied in his reckless fall from grace;
I countered with new hope's divine plan,
Which rescues and prepares for us a place.

Despite the terrible clash of forces,
I felt secure with each swing of my sword;
The demon's power came from dark sources,
But mine was greater…it comes from the Lord.

Thus, I banished the monster to the pit,
His final screams left ringing in my ears;
The manor's servants took control of it,
Charged with ushering in more peaceful years.

My quest is complete…my work never done,
Yet for the night, I will now take my rest;
I'll rise once again with the morning sun
And go forth to conquer the next day's test.

The Priest's Tale

When fools rush in where angels fear to tread,
God sends special angels to walk the Earth…
Special men and women to ease the dread
And remind you of your ultimate worth.

I come bearing blessings and gifts of love
To give to all souls, from greatest to least;
I'm a citizen of the realms above,
But known to my earthly friends as a priest.

For the sick, there is healing in my hands,
And the hungry shall receive blessed bread;
For the souls without hope in distant lands,
I offer life rising up from the dead.

With the power of God, I take my stand
Against the evil one's wicked deceit;
By His word, I admonish and rebuke
Each dark spirit to ensure its defeat.

I bring together kingdoms and nations,
Encouraging them to lay down the sword
And embrace as men of common station,
United by God and His holy word.

All I ask is an open mind and ear,
And a heart that is willing to believe
In a God who desires to draw near,
With blessings and love for you to receive.

The Rogue's Tale

The shadows are my friend…I need none else,
For my craft is one that you may not like;
If you're my target, you wouldn't know it,
Until the moment when I choose to strike.

Don't assume to know me, because you don't…
I am many faces and none at all;
The face you see is what I choose to show,
Whenever I choose it…that is my call.

I take that which I fancy…nothing more,
Yet thievery is but a single piece
Of my life's puzzle…no, you can't solve it
Without chasing those elusive wild geese.

My motives aren't all material;
I simply take joy in creating strife
By taking whatever treasures I find,
Whether money, one's virtue…or one's life.

I never sleep without one eye open,
Lest I hasten the eventual day
When I too will suffer the fate of fools
And find my own treasures plundered away.

The shadows are my friend...but I'm not theirs,
Because the game is never mine to win;
Some day, my turn will come to pay the price
Of ultimate devotion to my sin.

The Sorcerer's Tale

The universe is filled with mysteries…
As many as there are stars in the sky;
I've spent a lifetime seeking to learn them
As my role in Eternity speeds by.

I am called a variety of names:
To some, I am "wizard;" to others, "mage;"
I'm simply a student of mysteries,
Seeking answers with each turn of a page.

While others embrace swords, or gods, or guile,
I seek the energies of time and space;
Mystic forces flow through this open vessel
And out again to make a better place.

There is much more to what most call "magic"
Than waving wands or intoning phrases;
Only the disciplined intellect grasps
That true knowledge is obtained in stages.

The masses fear what they don't understand,
And shun secret truths which they cannot hold;
Thus, my mystical musings are hidden,
Lest fools try to become wise, and turn bold.

Natural force is not summoned lightly;
Those who dare to try and swallow it whole
Will themselves be swallowed without a trace,
Leaving the remains of a shattered soul.

Instead, by touching the hem of the cloak
Woven from the fabric of time and space,
I sip gently from the arcane fountain
And am filled with supernatural grace.

As the sands in my life's hourglass run,
I go on finding mysteries to solve;
Each new question a touch of the fabric…
Each answer allowing me to evolve.

The Warrior's Tale

My favorite color of all is red…
The red of the sun in the sky at dawn,
It brings to mind the heartbeats full of blood
That will soon be drunk by the castle lawn.

The love of my life is a blade of steel…
Her dazzling smile betrays a wanton lust
For the song of combat along the side
Of the only one to command her trust.

Is it not a glorious day to die?
Each day I renew my courtship of Death,
Whether by Man or monster, I flourish
In a fight where I could take my last breath.

Let the weak ones use their magical tricks,
It matters not the subtle wizard's guile;
My love's caress between his shoulder blades
Will undoubtedly serve to cramp his style.

Let the cowardly ones strike from behind,
For such rogues will learn of the awesome speed
As my mistress splits them from stem to stern;
Learn this lesson well, and always take heed.

My favorite color of all is red…
The red of the sun in the sky at dusk,
It matches the hue of the fleeting blood
That spills from my soon-to-be lifeless husk.

Is it not a glorious day to die?
My courtship of Death will soon be complete,
My soul will depart for Valhalla's shores,
And with long-dead fellows, I'll take my seat.

Printed in the United States
25438LVS00001B/118-135